Blizzard Bluster!

❄ SpongeBob's Book of Frosty Funnies ❄

ISBN-13: 978-0-545-03887-4
ISBN-10: 0-545-03887-1

12 11 10 9 8 7 6 5 4 3 2 1   7 8 9 10 11 12/0

Printed in the U.S.A.
First Scholastic printing, September 2007

Blizzard Bluster!

SpongeBob's Book of Frosty Funnies

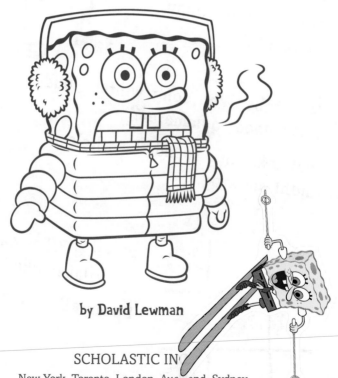

by David Lewman

SCHOLASTIC INC.

New York Toronto London Auckland Sydney

Mexico City New Delhi Hong Kong Buenos Aires

How did SpongeBob pick his favorite flake?

"Eeny, meeny, miny, snow . . ."

Mr. Krabs: Why don't winter clouds make good roommates?

Patrick: They spend the whole night snowing.

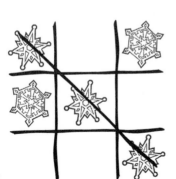

Patrick: What game do snowflakes like best?

SpongeBob: Tic-tac-snow

Squidward: What did the starter say in the race between two winter clouds?

Sandy: "Ready, set, snow!"

Squidward: Knock, knock.
SpongeBob: Who's there?
Squidward: Snow.
SpongeBob: Snow who?
Squidward: 'S no way I'm going out in that cold, wet stuff.

5

Did the huge snowstorm do much damage in Bikini Bottom?

No, everything turned out all white.

Mrs. Puff: Who's great at painting and is always cold?

Squidward: Vincent van Snow.

How did Patrick feel when he saw the new snowfall?

It was love at first white.

Pearl: Why did the piece of ice break up with the piece of snow?

Plankton: He turned out to be a real flake.

SpongeBob: What do you get when you cross cereal with snow?

Patrick: Corn flakes.

FLAKES

Sandy: What's Patrick's favorite thing to eat in the winter?

Mr. Krabs: Cold slaw.

Pearl: What did the snowwoman do when the snowman asked her out?

Mrs. Puff: She gave him the cold shoulder.

Mr. Krabs: What do you get when you slice lunch meat during a snowstorm?

Plankton: Cold cuts.

Brrr! Brrr! Brrr! Brrr!

Why didn't Patrick perform in the ice show?

He got cold feet.

Brrr!

Brrr!

9

Why couldn't Sandy follow the Alaskan Bull Worm through the snow?

The trail had gone cold.

Patrick: Knock, knock.
SpongeBob: Who's there?
Patrick: Scold.
SpongeBob: Scold who?
Patrick: 'S cold out here, isn't it?

Why did Plankton bring a hammer to the skating party?

He wanted to break the ice.

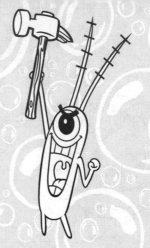

Why did Patrick try to lick the freezing pond?

He'd heard it was icing.

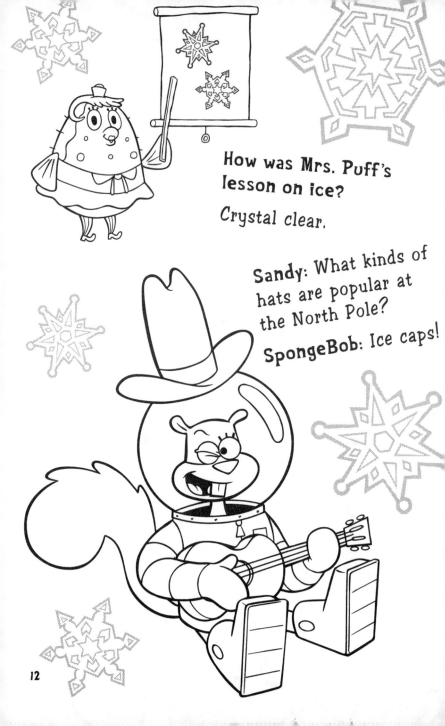

How was Mrs. Puff's lesson on ice?

Crystal clear.

Sandy: What kinds of hats are popular at the North Pole?

SpongeBob: Ice caps!

Patrick: Why were the snowflakes all dressed up?

SpongeBob: They were going to a crystal ball.

What do young snowballs like to play at recess?

Freeze tag.

What happened when the Dirty Bubble tried to act in the ice show?

He froze up.

What do you get when you cross Sandy's tree with a pile of snow?

Driftwood.

Patrick: Do snowflakes make good students?

Mrs. Puff: No, they keep drifting off.

Sandy: Was the snowfall a big hit in Bikini Bottom?

Mrs. Puff: Yes, it took the town by storm.

What did Patrick sing as he ran into the snowstorm?

"We're off to see the blizzard!"

Why did Sandy jump on a jellyfish during the blizzard?

She wanted to ride out the storm.

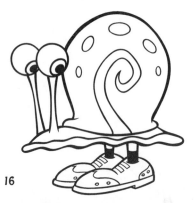

Sandy: When are shoes like an icy sidewalk?

SpongeBob: When they're slip-ons!

How did Patrick do on his skating test?

He slipped by.

What happened when the cops chased Man Ray onto the ice?

He gave 'em the slip.

Brrr! Brrr! Brrr! Brrr! Brrr!

How did SpongeBob score a run during the snowstorm?

He slid home!

Why did Patrick walk to work with SpongeBob on the icy day?

He just went along for the slide.

What is SpongeBob's favorite snowy day game?

Slide-and-seek.

Why did Patrick cry loudly during the blizzard?

He wanted to make a snow bawl.

19

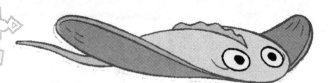

SpongeBob: What has a carrot nose and glides through the ocean?

Squidward: A snow-manta ray.

Pearl: What did the snowflake say to the sidewalk?

SpongeBob: "Let's stick together."

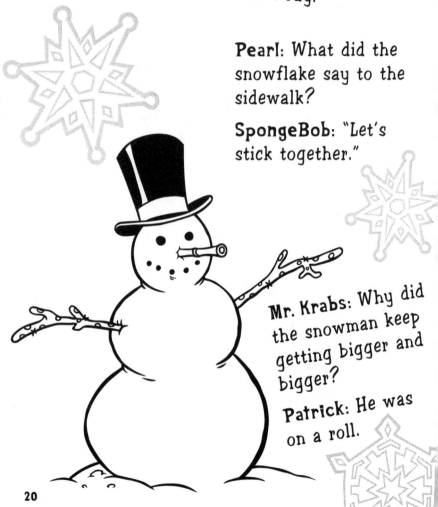

Mr. Krabs: Why did the snowman keep getting bigger and bigger?

Patrick: He was on a roll.

SpongeBob: What happens when snowmen get mad?

Mr. Krabs: They have a total meltdown.

How did the snowman know he loved Patrick's grill?

When he saw it, he melted.

Barnacleboy: What do snowmen like to do on hot days?

Mermaidman: Chill out.

What did SpongeBob say to the snowman going to Mussel Beach?

"Have a nice drip!"

Brrr!
Brrr!
Brrr!
Brrr!
Brrr!

Patrick: Why don't snowmen ride bikes?

SpongeBob: They hate to puddle.

Brrr!

Brrr!

Brrr!

Brrr!

Patrick: Are snow sandwiches good?

SpongeBob: Yes, they melt in your mouth.

Sandy: What did the snowman wear to the hot office?

Mrs. Puff: A wet suit.

Mr. Krabs: Did the rising temperatures make the snowmen leave Bikini Bottom?

Mrs. Puff: Yes, it was the last thaw.

Barnacleboy: Who wears a mask and steals ice and snow?

Mermaidman: A *brrr*-glar.

Sandy: What do you get when you cross a donkey and a glacier?

Squidward: A *brrr*-o.

What does Patrick
use to slide down
a snowy hill?

A SpongeBobsled!

Why was Squidward
grouchy after he
tried tobogganing?

He got up on the
wrong side of
the sled.

How did SpongeBob feel when he went off the ski ramp?

Jumpy!

What did Sandy do when SpongeBob suggested they try the ski ramp?

She jumped at the chance!

Mrs. Puff: Which fish moves best on the ice?

Mr. Krabs: The skate.

SpongeBob: Why did the parrot go to the skating rink?

Painty the Pirate: To play ice squawky.

How did Patrick score
a goal in his very first
hockey match?

Beginner's puck.

Why did Mr. Krabs
want to join the
hockey team?

He heard he got to
chase a buck.

Brrr!

Squidward: Which bird is best at hockey?

Sandy: The seagoal.

Brrr!

What's the coldest thing SpongeBob puts in a Krabby Patty?

Iceberg lettuce.

Brrr!

What did the snowman say when Plankton stole his nose?

"See if I carrot!"

Squidward: What did the math teacher make after the blizzard?

Mrs. Puff: Snow angles.

Brrr! Brrr! Brrr! Brrr!

SpongeBob: How do you find a duck in the snow?

Sandy: Follow his quacks.

Why did Patrick lie on the wall of snow?

SpongeBob told him to hold down the fort.

Patrick: Is cocoa bad?

SpongeBob: Yes, it's always getting into hot water.

Mr. Krabs: What do electric eels drink on snowy days?

Plankton: Hot *shock*olate.

SpongeBob: Was the cocoa mad at the marshmallows?

Patrick: No, he was just letting off steam.

Mr. Krabs: Which dog keeps you warm in the winter?

Sandy: An Irish Sweater.

How did the snowman feel when SpongeBob covered him in coal?

He got a lump in his coat.

Patrick: What did the two fingers do on the cold day?

Pearl: They fell in glove.

Why did SpongeBob think he was fired on the snowy day?

Mr. Krabs gave him the boots.

Mr. Krabs: What do bakers wear on cold days?

SpongeBob: Ear muffins.

Sandy: What did the daddy truck say to the baby truck on the snowy day?

Squidward: "Why don't you go outside and plow?"

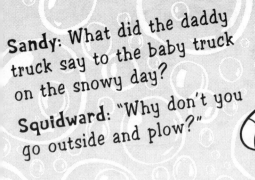

SpongeBob: Why do teeth talk so much on a cold day?

Patrick: They can't stop chattering.

Mrs. Puff: What's the best grade to get on a freezing cold day?

Patrick: D-frost.

What happened to the Flying Dutchman when he sailed through the snowstorm?

He got a terrible case of frostboat.

Sandy: What do you use to catch frozen fish?

Mr. Krabs: Frostbait.

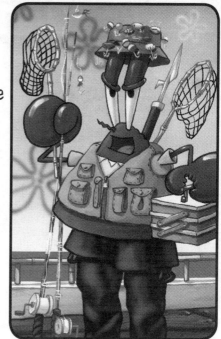

What's the difference between having your fingers frozen and being scared of Mr. Krabs?

One's a case of frostbite, and the other's a case of boss fright.

Brrr!

Brrr!

Sandy: When is a dog like a chilly day?

Plankton: When it's nippy.

Brrr!

Brrr!

Why did Plankton stay outside through an entire blizzard?

He wanted to be king of the chill.

Brrr!

Brrr!

Patrick: Which cold breeze is the smartest?

Squidward: A sharp wind.

Brrr!

Brrr!

Why did Patrick drag his bed out into the blizzard?

He'd heard there were sheets of ice and a blanket of snow.

Brrr!

Why did Mr. Krabs go digging for money in the drift?

He'd heard it was a snow bank.

Why do the coldest customers get their Krabby Patties first?

Because it's first numb, first served.

Sandy: Which skating move do gorillas do best?

Squidward: The figure ape.

Painty the Pirate: Which pirate is the coldest?

The Flying Dutchman: Ahrr, that be Bluebeard!

43

What's **Mr. Krabs's** favorite **frozen** treat?

Snow coins.

Why did Pearl stick her face in the fresh snow?

She wanted to powder her nose.

SpongeBob: What do you get when you cross an oyster with fresh snow?

Mr. Krabs: Clam powder.

Patrick: Why did the little snowflake rise from the ground?

SpongeBob: His mom told him to flurry up.

Squidward: Which sea serpent moves best through a blizzard?

Plankton: A snowmob-eel.

SpongeBob: When is snow ready to travel in a ball?

Patrick: When it's all packed.

Mr. Krabs: What do you call a hog pen made out of ice?

Sandy: A pigloo.

Patrick: What did the mama ice say to the little boy ice?

SpongeBob: "That's enough of your wisecracks!"

SNAP!

Chill out!

(We're done.)